AF355542

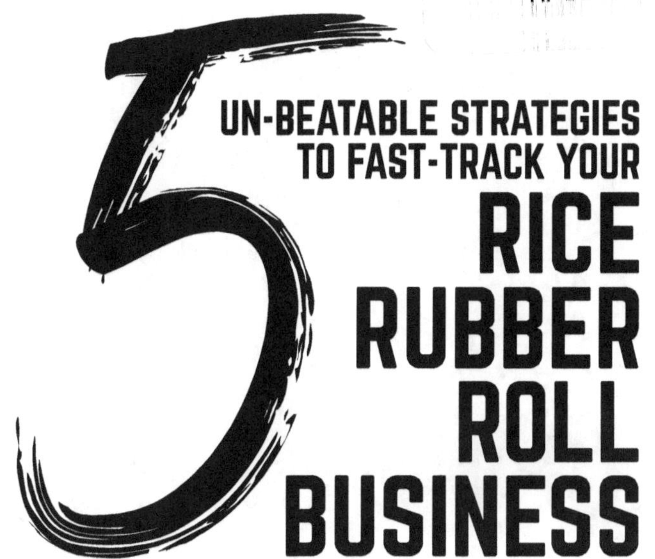

5
UN-BEATABLE STRATEGIES
TO FAST-TRACK YOUR
RICE
RUBBER
ROLL
BUSINESS

AMIT GARG

Worldwide Published by
 Pendown Press

PENDOWN PRESS

An ISO 9001 & ISO 14001 Certified Co.,
Regd. Office: 2525/193, 1st Floor, Onkar Nagar-A,
Tri Nagar, Delhi-110035
Ph.: 09350849407, 09312235086
E-mail: info@pendownpress.com
Branch Office: 1A/2A, 20, Hari Sadan, Ansari Road,
Daryaganj, New Delhi-110002
Ph.: 011-45794768
Website: PendownPress.com

First Edition: 2021

ISBN: 978-93-91544-03-4

Layout and Cover Designed by Pendown Graphics Team
Printed and Bound in India by Thomson Press India Ltd.

DEDICATION

This book is my humble and loving tribute to my Father, Late Shri Shyam Lal Garg, who left me the legacy of this Rice Rubber Roll Business and the legacy of human values such as integrity, compassion, and honesty.

CONTENTS

ACKNOWLEDGEMENTS

Though written by me, this book wouldn't have been possible without the support of each and every member of my staff at the office, in the factory, and on the sales team. The Hindustan Group is at the top of our industry because of all of you. I take this opportunity to express heartfelt gratitude for you all.

This whole project would be incomplete if I did not express my sincere thanks to my mentor Mr.Akshar Yadav for inspiring and motivating me to be better and do better and encouraging me to share my vast expertise and learning to help others become more profitable and successful.

ABOUT ME

Hello, I am Amit Garg. I am a science graduate from Hindu College, Delhi University and have received a MASTERS degree from the Indian Rubber Institute in technical up-gradation of Rubber products. I am the Director of Hindustan Rubber Industries, one of the leading firms in the rice mill industry. The rice rubber roll industry is growing rapidly and will continue to grow in the future. My mission is to help dealers/distributors grow their business by following some very simple and easy steps. And this intent would help us as a unit to grow to the next level. I have done my best in using my technical background and education to make one of the finest qualities of RICE RUBBER ROLLS & PHENOL FORMALDEHYDE RESINS (a Key ingredient in making rubber rolls).

The paddy industry is getting more competitive every day. As a result, new players are entering the market, and those who don't innovate are stagnating and losing market share.

The question is: Are you doing enough to attract, convert & retain your customers to stay on top?

Did you know that above 95% of Rice Rubber Roll Distributors are suffering because of stagnant sales, squeezing profits & growing bad debt?

The most interesting aspect of the above problem is that 99% of the above problem is only due to 5 major causes.

Just address these 5 causes and nothing can stop your phenomenal rise in this industry.

For the last 35 years, the Hindustan Group has maintained its position as the MOST RELIABLE SOURCE to buy Rice Rubber Rolls, PAN India – with loyal customers worldwide.

In this book, I will share 5 sure-shot strategies to have a never-ending flow of lucrative customers and escalate your business growth.

(These are my tried and tested methods that have delivered exceptional results & made us India's industry experts.) Following and implementing these five strategies is guaranteed to help you improve your business volume, enhance your profitability radically and thereby make more money.

#1 UNDERSTAND THE SIGNIFICANCE OF YOUR PRODUCT RANGE & RELATED PRODUCTS

The most complex part of the distribution is customer acquisition. It takes all the hard work in the world to acquire and win the trust of a customer. However, since you have already invested time, money and energy into nurturing your customer, and you have a ready customer base. It would be a shame not to leverage this advantage by selling them your other related products with the same amount of effort. Using this strategy creates a win-win situation for both you and your customer. You have the option of multiplying your business many fold with the same amount of effort and your customer has the option of finding more products under one umbrella from a source they already trust. This minimizes their effort and gives them more value too.

Let's understand this more clearly through the following two examples:

When Apple sells laptops to a customer, it is very easy for them to sell related products such as printers, headphones and speakers as well. Now, whatever effort they have put in was to get the customer to buy the laptop from them. Once the customer buys the laptop, they have a ready customer base. Now they can sell the related products like printers, speakers etc. to the same customer without any extra effort or expenditure thus multiplying their business with minimum cost. The customer is also delighted because they get the same assured quality at one stop.

Now lets understand this specifically in terms of our industry. In our case, wherever we use rice rubber rolls, whitener stones/abrasives are also required to separate the bran layer from the rice (since whitener stones/abrasive cones remove the extra layer of bran on the rice and give it a whitish look.) Thus these two sets of products can easily be sold together to the customer with the same amount of effort that selling one product would take.

For example, our dealer in Bangladesh was earlier selling only Rubber Rolls for many years. We suggested that he start recommending and pitching the whitener stones also to the customers who bought Rice Rubber Rolls. After adding our Whitener Stones to his product mix, he has now started a full range of Modern Rice Machinery Parts showroom. This has resulted in increased profits and stronger customer loyalty with the same amount of effort and expenditure.

Hindustan Group is a pioneer in manufacturing different whitener stone abrasive cones used in rice mills.

Stone/cone is a very delicate item because, technically, it is glass. Therefore, utmost care must be taken while handling and supplying it. Also, since its consumption is not as big as rice rubber rolls, buying in bulk or an FCL 20 feet container is not always practical. Therefore here is a PRO-TIP that will make this strategy work for you.

Key Strategy: Use Joint Shipping

How We Do It

Since we manufacture both rice rubber rollers & whitener stones, we ship some quantities of whitener stones with rice rubber rollers to our foreign buyers.

By shipping both items together, we reduce costs and make safe as well as timely deliveries.

#2 DEVELOP EXCELLENT PRODUCT KNOWLEDGE & EDUCATE YOUR CUSTOMERS

To sell well, you must know your products inside out. Without proper product knowledge, you won't be able to communicate your product's USP to your customers. When you speak about your products to your customers they must be able to feel the passion and the depth of knowledge that you have. Only when they perceive you as an expert will they trust you completely.

Building this trust and confidence in your customers is only possible when you know your products like the back of your hand. There is no shortcut to this. You will have to make the effort to master your product knowledge to be able to generate excitement, enthusiasm, interest and confidence in your customers towards the products you sell. This works like magic to actually closing sales deals.

(The other day, while I was sitting at my publisher 'friend's office. I curiously asked him – How do you rate the profitability of your products (in his case, books)? His reply was simple yet filled with confidence. He said, "Amit, if you are ready and willing to pay the money that's printed as the cost of your book, then you need not worry about its sale."). This was an awesome insight; to sell my book, I had to believe in it first.

'Here's the thing. If you don't believe in what you are selling, neither will your customers.'

Key Strategy: Always Educate Your Customers

For a business to be successful, your intent should always be to help the customer and add value to their life/business. Knowing your product masterfully will allow you to show your customers how your product solves their problem and delivers excellent results.

How We Do It

Since both our products are entirely related and have the same customer base,we have hired a dedicated R&D team to solve problems faced in Rice Mills.

We work hard to ensure that this expert team provides detailed product knowledge to our dealers and distributors, answers their questions and helps them grow their business.

#3 SOURCE THE BEST QUALITY PRODUCTS FROM REPUTED BRANDS

The most crucial part of our rice rubber roller business, or any business for that matter, is the product itself. The product is the center or the Hero of any and every business. Remember, all products are not the same.

For example, even though all cars run on four wheels, they are all different. So now to run a flourishing and constantly growing business, the biggest challenge is finding the best product. The biggest challenge is how to find a product from the best possible source?

For example, in our rice rubber roll industry, the four main options to buy products are:

- India
- China
- Vietnam
- Local Manufacturer

Now, you may find cheap product sources and inferior products flooding the market, but are they the best option for sustained long-term success and profitability?

Key Strategy: Invest In High-Quality Products & Reliable Partners Only

I, Amit Garg and the team have successfully established the Hindustan Group as the leading supplier and authority figure of rice rubber rolls in India.

Our customers know they can count on us and with good reason

How We Do It

Openness and Transparency: India is the world's biggest democracy and an open economy. And this characteristic reflects in our businesses too.

In India, no one can introduce an overnight law to stop any business. However, this can happen in other countries. Take, for example, the case of Mr Jack Ma, the founder of Alibaba, who was penalized for his comments against the government.

Trust: When our customer buys products from us, their purchase decision reflects their trust and faith in us as a reputed supplier of Rice Rubber Rolls.

We consistently build our customers' trust by keeping our commitments, no matter what the circumstances. As a result, our customers vouch for our product quality, service quality and reliability. This is possible only because we choose to associate with the best quality products and reliable, customer and service oriented partners.

We are always there to help our customers and attend to their feedback and complaints promptly.

Let me share a CASE STUDY about how we went the extra mile to help a customer and won their trust.

BACKGROUND: One of our customers was engaged in raw paddy milling. As he expanded and received orders for parboiled rice, he began milling parboiled paddy.

Since he was regularly purchasing rice rubber rolls and whitener stones for raw paddy from us, we were in regular touch. However, after starting boiled paddy milling, he faced a peculiar problem.

THE CHALLENGE: While whitening the rice, the screen of the whitener stone would choke very quickly. This led to rejections as only negligible air passed in the system, increasing the temperature of both the rice and whitener stone. Now, the quality of the rice became poor, and there was an increase in the percentage of broken rice.

Not able to find a solution, he called me to discuss his problem.

THE SOLUTION: My team and I immediately sprang into action, and within 12 hours, we gave our customer a winning solution!

We suggested injecting a certain quality of husk along with rice into the whitening machine, and it immediately solved his problem.

He then asked me what was the reason for the problem and how putting husk into the machine resolved the issue?

WHY DID IT WORK? While boiling paddy, the oil content of the rice comes to the surface. The bran layer is very sticky, and when the stone removes this layer of bran, it easily sticks onto the screen's surface.

So, when we put some husk into the system, the husk acts as a cleaner and abrasive. It removes the sticky bran layer from the screen and opens its air gaps.

***

With countries, too, trust is developed by helping smaller countries, not harassing them. However, we can see this is not happening in some cases.

#4 INNOVATE AND ESTABLISH CREDIBILITY

Trust is never random, it is built up over time and comes from your experience and reach.

For example, if a particular doctor or surgeon has been doing surgeries for thirty years, nobody will doubt his credibility. Similarly, India is the 2nd largest producer of rice with a wide range from very long grain to very short grain. Thus India is in itself a name synonymous with credibility in the Rice industry.

To add to the stamp of Indian Credibility there are various other factors that we have worked hard at to ensure that our customers trust us completely.

A Vast Dealership Network: At the Hindustan Group, we have a dealership of over 250 dealers all over India, and we are known for being reliable. This network has been built with tremendous sincere efforts and detailed care for our customers and partners.

R&D: Innovation is our middle name. Whenever we manufacture a new customized product, we test run the product on our domestic rice mill & start production only after perfecting the product. We are very careful about launching the product only when all the snags have been worked out. We believe in researching the market and its needs thoroughly and then on working to develop solutions to address those needs.

Key Strategy: Perform Thorough Research, Then Introduce Excellent Products

How We Do It

Our product, New Age Rice Rubber Roll 2.0, sells like hotcakes the world over, not just due to its exceptionally high life (output) but also because its hardness is below the industry average. So, 0% noise and 0% vibration while the rolls work.

Our expert R&D makes these features possible through their tireless efforts. They constantly worked hard and gathered feedback from our numerous customers to make this MAGIC happen!

Additionally, our product named 1121 gives outstanding results as long grain rice like Basmati 1121. Since in India long-grain rice is produced in large quantities, our product 1121 sells in large numbers all over the country.

And New Age Rubber Roll 2.0 sells in large quantities Internationally since, in most countries, short-grain rice is more prominently grown.

#5 INVEST IN THE RIGHT MARKETING

People who wait for customers to come to them are the ones who are satisfied with their business, but people who wish to grow don't wait for the customer to come to them. Instead, they reach out to them.

After sourcing products from a good source, the next big thing you need to do to run a sustainable and growing business is the Right Marketing.

So many times, we have observed that in a business, things are moving slowly, and the business is either stagnating or losing its foothold. However, when a new person joins the company, such as the son/daughter or a new senior executive, the company starts to grow in fast-forward mode with the same products.

Do you know the only different thing added to the business? It is the Right Marketing approach!

Here's the thing. We, humans, make a common mistake, even in our personal life. Which is that we STOP treating our wife like we did when she was our girlfriend.

The same is true for our business also. When we either start a new business or add a new customer, we care for them from the bottom of our hearts. But as time passes, we become careless towards them and begin taking them for granted.

Key Strategy: Never Stop Marketing And Do It Right

How We Do It

Good Marketing involves being in touch with your customers consistently. We follow many ways to stay in contact with our cherished clients and customers – such as Email, WhatsApp, Phone Calls, and Meeting them in person.

We send clients valuable information weekly by email/ WhatsApp. These include product testimonials, latest achievements, new technology updates, products related to the rice mill industry and more.

(To know more about how you can market your business, do check out the Book of Marketing Guru, Mr Akshar Yadav, by the name of SELL IN BULK.)

I am sure that if you follow the 5 Power-Packed Strategies i have shared in this book, you will set new records of excellence in the paddy business. New, profitable clients are within reach! Go out and get them now!

We, the Hindustan Group, are leading manufacturers of Rice Rubber Rolls in India, currently manufacturing 1400 Rolls per day.

If you would like to understand the micro details of how these strategies work, feel free to Book a 1-2-1 ZOOM Session with me. I will be happy to help you.

IN A NUTSHELL

This book is to help dealers who wish to set up a new Rice Rubber Roll Distribution business or have an old setup but are unknowingly stuck in a stagnant business. By following above mentioned simple but consistent steps, one can really establish/grow a flourishing Rice Rubber Roll marketing setup.

I am always ready to help with all my resources to help dealers who wish to grow and do something better in life.

NEXT STEP

I have condensed my 35 years of experience into a few pages, and those who have believed in me have given very positive feedback. Some of the feedback are:-

I am genuinely proud to be associated with the Hindustan Group.

Dealer in PERU (South America)

My son is a changed personality and is now taking a very proactive role in the business and doing good. Thanks, Amit & your team.

Dealer in Punjab province (India).

CALL TO ACTION

This book has been written with the sole purpose of helping customers/friends who have faith in our company/ product. It gives you insight into how to improve things & take simple, basic steps to achieve your targets of more growth, higher sales volumes & multimillion-dollar profits.

If you wish to get more details, as if you are more hungry for knowledge & growth, you can book a one to one session with me on zoom/mail at **sales@hindustangroup.net** or **WhatsApp me @+91-9810029966.**

Please visit our website **www.hindustangroup.net** for more details.

Generally, my one-to-one sessions are overbooked, so in case there is some delay in booking, please forgive me in advance but be assured you will get a RESPONSE.